UKULELE CHORDS FOR KIDS

... & BIG KIDS TOO!

by Nancy Eriksson

A Fretted Friends Beginners Publication for Cabot Books

Published by:
Cabot Books

First Edition May 2016

ISBN-13: 978-1-906207-80-9

Cabot Books
3 Kenton Mews
Henleaze
Bristol
BS9 4LT
United Kingdom

Printed in The United States.

Visit our online site at www.frettedfriendsmusic.com
e-mail: cabotbooks@blueyonder.co.uk

CONTENTS

INTRODUCTION

Learning to play a musical instrument is a hobby that can last a lifetime. It can also lead to interesting career opportunities and into spheres such as teaching or part-time professional work.

Although some structured learning is needed by a beginner or intermediate student, the emphasis should still be to make music fun and not a daily chore to be endured rather than looked forward to. Young children in particular find it difficult to focus for long periods of time and if it feels too much like 'work', their interest will quickly fade. The days of sitting your bored 6-year-old in front of a piano and instructing them to practice their scales for the next hour are on the decline. For every child who benefits from this intense practice regime, another ten will be put off music altogether. On the flipside, if your child is engrossed in what he/she is doing, extended practice sessions are fine, within reason. But to generalise, 'less is more' within a learning environment, with plenty of encouragement thrown in to keep your child feeling positive regarding their progress.

The ukulele is a wonderful starter instrument for young children because of its small size, four soft nylon or composite strings and relatively low purchase price for a very playable instrument. As they progress, you can always upgrade to a better model. Much like the harmonica and recorder, the ukulele has developed an undeserved reputation as being little more than a child's toy. This is a long way from the truth, with professional quality ukes carrying four-figure price tags.

Despite only having four strings, the ukulele is still capable of playing complex five, six or seven note chords. This is achieved by omitting the less important parts within the chord, but retaining the fundamental 'color' of the sound. Even the guitar makes similar compromises despite having two further strings than the ukulele. To use a useful analogy, the eye doesn't need to see every inch of an elephant to know that it's an elephant. When it sees the trunk and the big ears, it knows what it is. Much the same reasoning is true regarding sound and harmony. The ear hears a thirteenth (a seven note chord), even if three of the notes are missing.

Good luck with your child's musical journey and remember music should always be fun!

UNDERSTANDING THE CHORD WINDOWS

The circle at the top indicates an open string is to be played. You don't need to use any fingers on your left hand to play an open string.

The arrow pointing to the number column shows you which frets are used playing a particular chord shape.

If you see an 'x' above a string in a chord window, it indicates the string shouldn't be played. Sometimes you might also see the 'x' directly on a string in the middle of a chord window. This tells you the string has to be damped using the pad on one your fingers directly above the string in question.

Most fingering positions will be dictated by where the notes are situated on the fingerboard. Others will be down to personal preference.

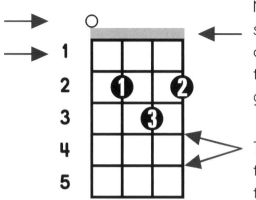

Nut Position indicating the chord should be played within the span of the first five frets. Beyond that, the nut is omitted from the diagram.

The frets. No chord window in this or any other book will contain a chord that spans any more than five frets.

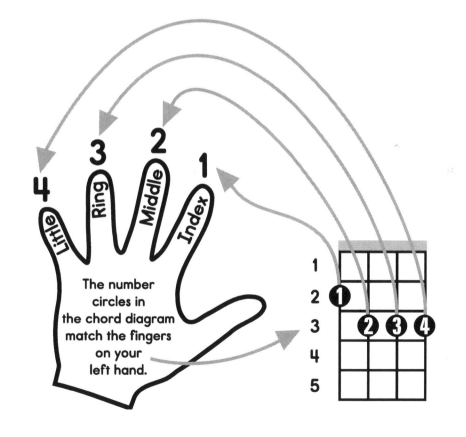

The number circles in the chord diagram match the fingers on your left hand.

5

ALL ABOUT CHORDS

Q: Does my young child need to learn chord theory?

A: Music is only enjoyable for young children if it's fun! So my advice would be to prioritise the 'hands on' approach and leave the more complex whys and hows until they're going to be receptive towards them. My one proviso being that they learn to use the chord window diagrams on their own. This also encourages the child to explore and achieve new sounds without the constant guidance of having an adult present.

Q: Should we skip this section of the book then?

A: Not necessarily. It may help if you can add some input yourself while your child is learning to play. The information is also accessible for older children and young adults.

Q: For how long should my child practice?

A: A young child shouldn't be playing for more than 30 minutes at a time unless they really want to. When playing becomes a chore, their interest is likely to wane. Physically, it can also be quite taxing on little fingers even with nylon or composite strings.

Q: What should I look for when buying a ukulele?

A: The criteria should be playability first and foremost. Check every fret on every string to make sure you don't get any buzz from them. Also pay careful attention to the 'action' (the height of the strings above the fingerboard/fretboard. If it takes a lot of pressing down, your child won't be able to properly play chords higher up the neck. It will also affect the intonation of the uke, making some chords sound out of tune. You don't have to spend a fortune to get a good starter instrument.

Q: What if he or she breaks a string?

A: Always keep a spare set in a drawer, as this is quite likely to happen from time to time. There are countless videos on YouTube and other sources showing how to put on a new string.

Q: How should I or my child tune the ukulele?

A: There are a variety of different ways to do this. Option 1: tune to a piano or electronic keyboard. This will pretty much ensure that you have the correct tuning. Option 2: use a chromatic tuner. These don't have to be particularly expensive, but you will have to replace batteries occasionally. Option 3: buy a set of pitch pipes designed for the ukulele. Not quite as accurate as the first two options, but a nice low tech solution for a child to blow and more fun than the other two.

Q: What is a chord?

A: It's a collection of three or more notes played at the same time.

Q: Are there any chords which break the rules on chord construction?

A: Yes. The 5th chord (C5, G5 etc.). Technically, this isn't a true chord as it only contains 2 intervals, a root and a fifth. But for the sake of convenience, it's allowed to gate crash the party and join the rest of it's musical cousins.

Q: What are intervals?

A: Intervals are the separate notes that make up a chord. The musical distance between each note tells you what type of chord it is. For example the chord of C major is a three note chord. It contains the notes C, E and G. The C is the first or 'root' note, the E is the 3rd note and the G is the 5th note (known as the 'Perfect Fifth'). To understand this better, try counting up the white notes from the 'C' on a piano keyboard.

Q: What is a triad?

A: A chord with three different notes in it. Examples include G (major), Bm (minor), D+ (augmented) and Asus4 (suspended fourth).

Q: What is a seventh?

A: It's an extra interval added to the end of a triad. There are many types of 7th chord, but the ones you'll use the most are the 'dominant' 7th and the 'major' 7th. Using the key of C as an example they will mainly be written as C7 (dominant) and Cmaj7 (major seventh).

Q: Which numbers aren't used in the naming of chords?

A: An 8th, a 10th and a 12th. All the others are used (1st or root, 2nd, 3rd, 4th, 5th, 6th, 7th, 9th, 11th and 13th. Some notes are also shared. The 2nd is the same note as a 9th, a 4th shares with the 11th and the 6th with the 13th. You can see this in action on the previous page.

Q: What is a chromatic scale?

A: It's a scale that includes all twelve notes featured in popular music. This includes all the white notes (the naturals) and black notes (sharps and flats) found a piano keyboard. Every chord in this book or any other piece of music includes a combination of some of these notes. The example below features the scale of C major.

| Root or 1st | Minor 2nd | Major 2nd | Minor 3rd | Major 3rd | Perfect 4th | Augmented 4th | *or* Diminished 5th | Perfect 5th | Minor 6th | Major 6th | Minor 7th | Major 7th |

Q: What is a ninth?

A: A ninth is a five note chord, consisting of a triad with the addition of a seventh and a ninth note. Again, it's most widely used types are the dominant ninth (for example, F9 or A9), the minor ninth (Dm9 or Fm9) and the major ninth (Dmaj9 or Bmaj9). In some instances the root, 3rd or 5th notes are omitted, depending on the chord. This doesn't greatly affect the overall sound, though.

Q: What is an extension?

A: A chord which goes beyond the scope of triads and sevenths. Basically, extensions are additional notes placed above the triad or seventh in a musical stave (or in piano terms, higher up the keyboard). These include 9ths, 11ths and 13ths in all their different incarnations. It's important to understand these are, for theoretical purposes, always placed above the seventh. Or in layman's terms higher up the scale. The confusion comes when you start to realise a 9th is identical to a 2nd (in the scale of C, a 'D' note).

Q: So why is the ninth note the same as the second note?

A: This takes a little grasping, but if you remember that if your note goes higher than the 7th, it's a ninth, but if it's lower, it'll be a 2nd. An example of this would be Csus2, which contains the root note of C, a 2nd or suspended D note and a G (the perfect fifth).

Q: So do other extensions share a note?

A: Yes. Other examples include the 11th (which is also a 4th) and the 13th (which shares a note with the 6th.

Q: Do elevenths and thirteenths have any particular properties?

A: Yes. In most cases the 3rd is omitted from eleventh chords and in turn, the 11th from the majority of thirteenths as they're deemed unnecessary and arguably create unwanted dissonance. In other instances the chords can be further truncated without changing the overall integrity of the sound.

Q: What is a suspended chord?

A: It's simpler to think of suspended chords as a stepping stone to a major or resolving chord. In effect the third has been left in a state of suspension by either raising it to a fourth (sus4) or lowering it to a second (sus2). Sevenths also provide versions of the suspended chord in the form of C7sus4 or E7sus2 (just to give two examples).

Q: What is a diminished chord?

A: A diminished chord has a dissonant quality to it where the third and fifth notes in a triad are flattened by a semi-tone. Again, using C as an example, C major (C-E-G) is altered to C° (C-E♭-G♭). A second version of a diminished chord is also used in many forms of music, the diminished seventh (e.g. C°7). This retains the elements of a standard diminished chord, adding a double flat in the seventh (C-E♭-G♭-B♭♭). A B♭♭ in this case is to all intents and purposes really an A note.

Q: What is an augmented chord?

A: An augmented chord basically performs the opposite task to a diminished one. Instead of lowering the fifth by a semi-tone, it raises it by the same interval. A C+ (augmented) chord contains the triad of C-E-G♯. The major root and third are retained and the fifth is sharpened.

Q: What is a sixth chord?

A: A sixth (or major sixth) is a major or minor triad with an added major sixth note. In the case of C6, it features the notes C-E-G-A. A sixth can also be minor, adding a gloomy quality to the chord. The only difference with the previous example is that the 3rd note is flattened. The resultant intervals would be C-E♭-G-A in the case of Cm6.

Q: What is a minor chord?

A: A minor chord, just like its major sibling is a triad. It always features the same root and fifth notes as a major chord, but takes on a more dramatic flavor by lowering or flattening the 3rd by a semi-tone. Cm includes the intervals of C-E♭-G (compared to C major, C-E-G). The other really important type of minor chord is the minor seventh. This is like a combination of the dominant seventh and the standard minor triad melded together. Both the 3rd and the 7th are flattened.

A typical minor seventh chord would be written Cm7, F#m7 or Am7, just to give three different examples.

Q: What is an added chord?

A: It's a note or notes that are added to a basic chord to create a generally fuller sound. A prime example of this would be the added ninth chord. Here, the basic triad is supplemented by the addition of a ninth. So again, going back to C major (C-E-G), when you add the ninth, it becomes Cadd9 (expressed in intervals as C-D-E-G). This chord can also be written as Cadd2, depending on whether it's viewed by the composer as a major second (Cadd2) or a ninth (Cadd9). Either way, it's the same chord. Other popular added chords include a minor version of the triad with an added interval (Cmadd9 or Cmadd2). This is a basic minor chord with the major second or ninth added (C-D-Eb-G in the case Cmadd9 or Cadd2).

Q: What are inversions?

A: In the root version of a chord, the notes run in their correct order from lowest to highest. In the case of G major, it would be G-B-D. With an inversion of the same chord, the notes would run in a different order. For example, the 1st inversion of G major would be B-D-G and the 2nd, D-G-B. In general, triads sound more or less the same when they're inverted. This becomes less true though, as the chords become more complex. Take a Cmaj7 (major seventh) chord in it's root position (C-E-G-B). It has a gentle relaxed feeling to it. Then move it up to the 1st inversion and it suddenly takes on a slightly unpleasant dissonant quality. Another interesting example of a clear sonic difference between the root note and one of its inversions is C6 (C-E-G-A). When you move up to its 3rd inversion, you're basically playing the chord of Am7, which sounds quite different from a major sixth chord.

Q: Some chords are called by different names in different music books. What should we do?

A: The alternative chord names reference chart on page 13 should sort out the confusion. The examples are in the key of C, but equally apply to all twelve keys.

UKULELE QUESTIONS

Q: What is reentrant tuning?

A: It's a tuning that doesn't run in a regular high to low sequence.   With most fretted instruments the highest notes are generally furthest away from the player's chin, with each subsequent string lowering in tone. In the case of the guitar, the lowest sounding string, the 'E' is nearest to the player's chin. With the ukulele, its most popular tuning breaks with this formula and instead of the 4th and final string ('G') getting lower, it raises up to a high 'G' instead. This is reentrant tuning. Some players prefer a more regular method of tuning, though and lower the 'G' instead. The mnemonic, 'my dog has fleas' is a great way of remembering how to tune the ukulele using reentrant tuning. The ukulele isn't the only instrument to deploy reentrant tuning. Other examples include the bluegrass 5-string banjo and the charango.

Q: How many members of the ukulele family are there?

A: The most popular model is undoubtedly the soprano (or standard uke), which is generally tuned G4-C4-E4-A4 (the numbers represent standard scientific pitch notation, with every number indicating which octave the note belongs to). The best instrument to demonstrate how the numbers run, is on a standard 88-note piano keyboard. The lowest note ('A') is designated A0 and the highest, ('C') C8. Other popular models in the family include the 'concert' uke which uses the same tuning, followed by the bigger tenor uke, which adds a further tuning to its repetoire (D3-G3-B3-E4) as well as the popular G4-C4-E4-A4. All three also employ non-reentrant tuning as well. The soprano and tenor also use the higher A4-D4-F#4-B4 popularised in the first half of the twentieth century. Finally, the other standard model within the family group is the baritone ukulele tuned to a G6 chord (D3-G3-B3-E4). Other non-standard members are occasionally produced including the sopranino, bass and contrabass ukuleles. Other loosely connected instruments include the Venezuelan cuatro, the cavaquinho, the charango, the timple and the American tiple.

Q: How many frets does a ukulele have?

A: A standard or soprano uke generally has no fewer than 12 frets and sometimes as many as 15. The concert and tenor, between 15 and 19 and the baritone 18-21. The larger instruments have a wider octave range when playing in positions higher up the neck.

ALTERNATIVE CHORD NAMES

C	**CM** or **Cmaj**	M	**major**
Cm	**Cmin** or **C-**	m	**minor**
C-5	**Cb5** or **C(b5)**	-	**minor**
C°	**Cdim**	dim	**diminished**
C5	**C Power Chord** or **C(no 3rd)**	°	**diminished**
Csus2	**C(sus2)** or **C2**	sus	**suspended**
Csus4	**Csus** or **C(sus4)**	aug	**augmented**
C+	**Caug, C+5** or **C(#5)**	+	**augmented**
C6	**CM6** or **CMaj6**	add	**added**
Cadd9	**Cadd2**	dom	**dominant**
Cm6	**C-6** or **Cmin6**	△	**delta / major seventh**
Cmadd9	**Cmadd2** or **C-(add9)**	#	**sharp**
C°7	**Cdim7**	✗	**double sharp**
C7	**Cdom**	b	**flat**
C7sus4	**C7sus, C7(sus4)** or **Csus11**	bb	**double flat**
C7-5	**C7b5**		
C7+5	**C7+** or **C7#5**		
C7-9	**C7b9** or **C7(addb9)**		
C7+9	**C7#9** or **C7(add#9)**		
Cm7	**C-7, Cmi7** or **Cmin7**		
Cm7-5	**Cm7b5** or **C-7-5**		
Cm(maj7)	**Cm#7, CM7-5, CmM7** or **C-△**		
Cmaj7	**CM7** or **C△(Delta)**		
C9	**C7(add9)**		
Cm9	**C-9** or **Cmin9**		
Cmaj9	**CM9, Cmaj7(add9), C△9** or **CM7(add9)**		
C11	**C7(add11)**		
C13	**C7/6(no 9th)** or **C7(add13)**		

The majority of music books will use the chords featured in the first column (on the far left), but should you come across alternatives, consult this guide for other naming conventions. The list on the right includes most of the symbols and abbreviations that you're likely to encounter in the majority of music books.

THE UKULELE FINGERBOARD LAYOUT

Fret | G | C | E | A

Fret				
1	G#Ab	C#Db	F	A#Bb
2	A	D	F#Gb	B
3	A#Bb	D#Eb	G	C
4	B	E	G#Ab	C#Db
5	C	F	A	D
6	C#Db	F#Gb	A#Bb	D#Eb
7	D	G	B	E
8	D#Eb	G#Ab	C	F
9	E	A	C#Db	F#Gb
10	F	A#Bb	D	G
11	F#Gb	B	D#Eb	G#Ab
12	G	C	E	A

4th   3rd   2nd   1st

Fingerboard note layout

The four notes across the top of the left-hand diagram represent the four open strings of a ukulele. If you stood the ukulele up on its bottom side facing you, the notes on the fingerboard would be identical to the diagram on the left.

When you reach the 12th fret the pattern repeats, again starting with GCEA. This is where the new octave starts on each string. An octave is a series of eight consecutive notes ending on the root note you started with. In the key of C, the intervals are C, D, E, F, G, A, B and C (all white notes). A complete octave will also include the semi-tones (a further five black notes). In other keys, it'll be a mixture of naturals, sharps and flats.

G   C   E   A

Ukulele GCEA tuning in standard notation

Note: the uke is written an octave lower than it sounds. The grey note on the 4th string represents the optional lower G tuning.

TUNING YOUR UKULELE

Reentrant Tuning.

Tuning the ukulele by fretting at different intervals on the fingerboard. The 4th 'G' string can be tuned in two different ways. The popular reentrant high 'G' tuning (left) or the low 'G' tuning (right). The lower G tuning will require a different gauge of string from the reentrant one, so bear this in mind when buying strings.

If you're playing with other people it's important that your ukulele is tuned accurately. With reentrant tuning, always tune the 3rd 'C' string first. With low G tuning, tune the 4th G string first.

Low G Tuning.

To tune your ukulele accurately, it's best to use an electronic chromatic tuner, but if there isn't one available, you can tune it to a guitar, piano/electronic keyboard or pitch pipes. The following tuning grid gives the correct fingering positions on the guitar fingerboard and piano keyboard.

Ukulele	Guitar	Piano
1st String (A)	1st string (E) fretted at the 5th fret	1st A above middle C
2nd String (E)	1st open string (E)	1st E above middle C
3rd String (C)	2nd string (B) fretted at the 1st fret	Middle C
4th String (G)	1st string (E) fretted at the 3rd fret	1st G above middle C
4th Low G String (G)	3rd open string (G)	1st G below middle C

C Chords

C5

C6

Cm6

Cmaj7

C Chords

Cadd9

Cmadd9

Cm7-5

C7sus4

C Chords

Csus2

Cm(maj7)

C7-5

C7+5

C Chords

C Chords

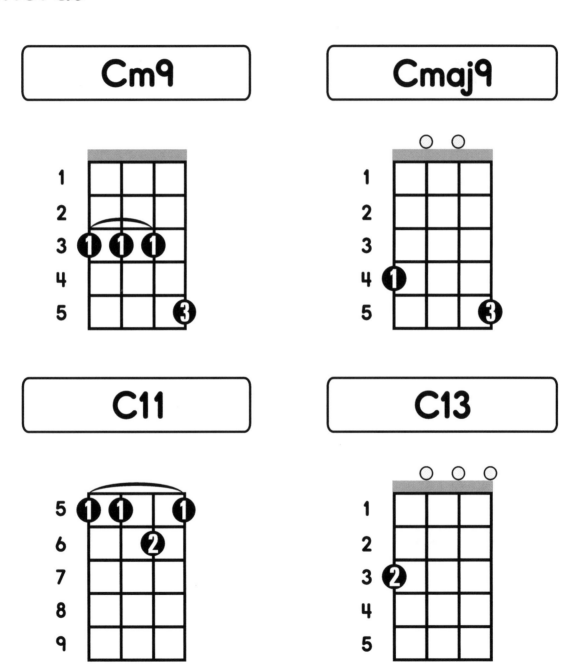

Db

Dbm

Db7

Dbm7

C# / D♭ Chords

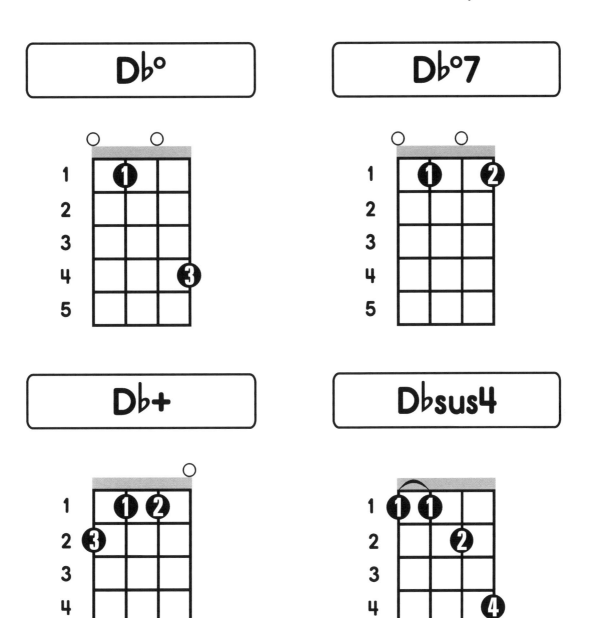

C# / Db Chords

Dbadd9

Dbmadd9

Dbm7-5

Db7sus4

D♭sus2

D♭m(maj7)

D♭7-5

D♭7+5

C# / D♭ Chords

D♭7-9

D♭7+9

D♭-5

D♭9

D♭m9

D♭maj9

D♭11

D♭13

D Chords

D Chords

D Chords

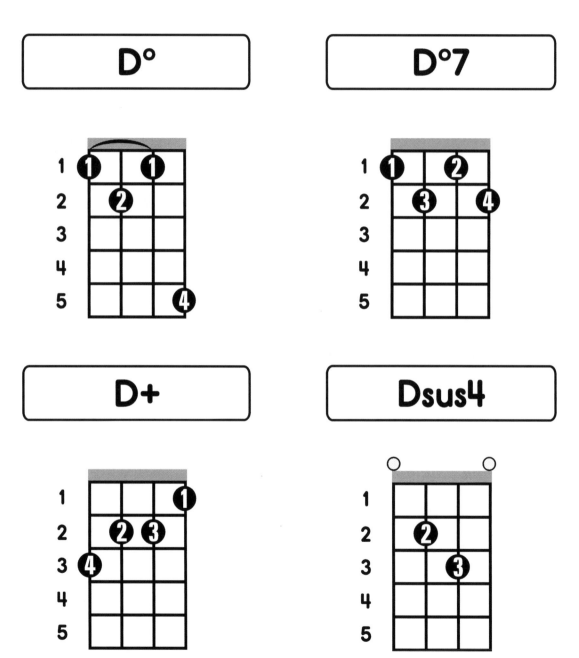

D Chords

Dadd9

Dmadd9

Dm7-5

D7sus4

33

D Chords

Dsus2

Dm(maj7)

D7-5

D7+5

D Chords

D Chords

Dm9

Dmaj9

D11

D13

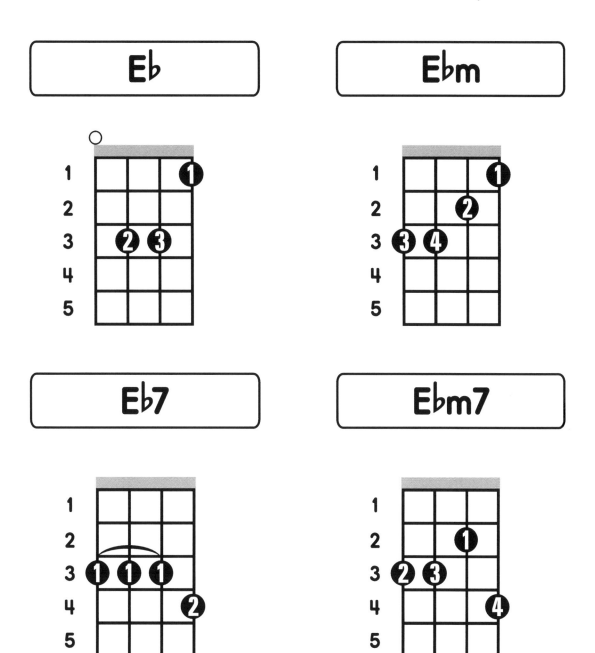

D# / E♭ Chords

E♭5

E♭6

E♭m6

E♭maj7

E♭°

E♭°7

E♭+

E♭sus4

D♯ / E♭ Chords

E♭add9

E♭madd9

E♭m7-5

E♭7sus4

D♯ / E♭ Chords

E♭sus2

E♭m(maj7)

E♭7-5

E♭7+5

D# / E♭ Chords

E♭7-9

E♭7+9

E♭-5

E♭9

E♭m9

E♭maj9

E♭11

E♭13

E Chords

E5

E6

Em6

Emaj7

E Chords

Eadd9

Emadd9

Em7-5

E7sus4

E Chords

Esus2

Em(maj7)

E7-5

E7+5

E Chords

E7-9

E7+9

E-5

E9

E Chords

F Chords

F Chords

F Chords

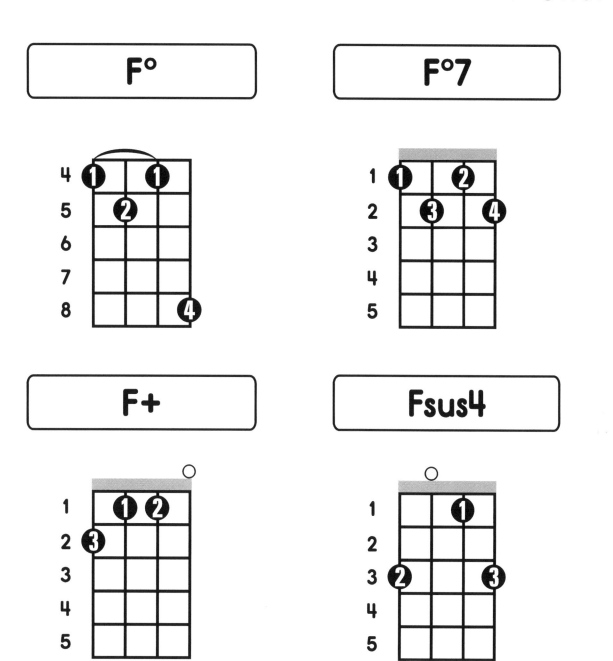

F Chords

Fadd9

Fmadd9

Fm7-5

F7sus4

F Chords

Fsus2

Fm(maj7)

F7-5

F7+5

F Chords

56

F Chords

Fm9

Fmaj9

F11

F13

F♯ / G♭ Chords

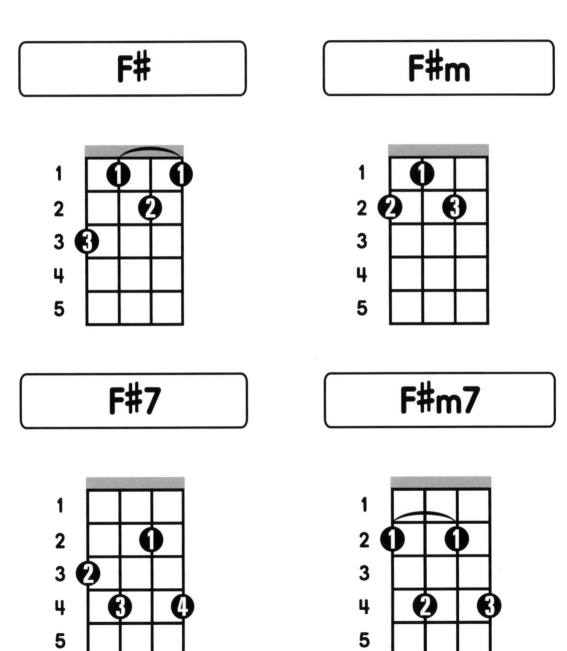

F# / G♭ Chords

F#5

F#6

F#m6

F#maj7

F# / Gb Chords

F#add9

F#madd9

F#m7-5

F#7sus4

F# / Gb Chords

F#sus2

F#m(maj7)

F#7-5

F#7+5

F# / G♭ Chords

F#7-9

F#7+9

F#-5

F#9

F# / G♭ Chords

F#m9

F#maj9

F#11

F#13

G Chords

G Chords

G Chords

G Chords

Gadd9

Gmadd9

Gm7-5

G7sus4

Gsus2

Gm(maj7)

G7-5

G7+5

G Chords

Gm9

Gmaj9

G11

G13

G# / A♭ Chords

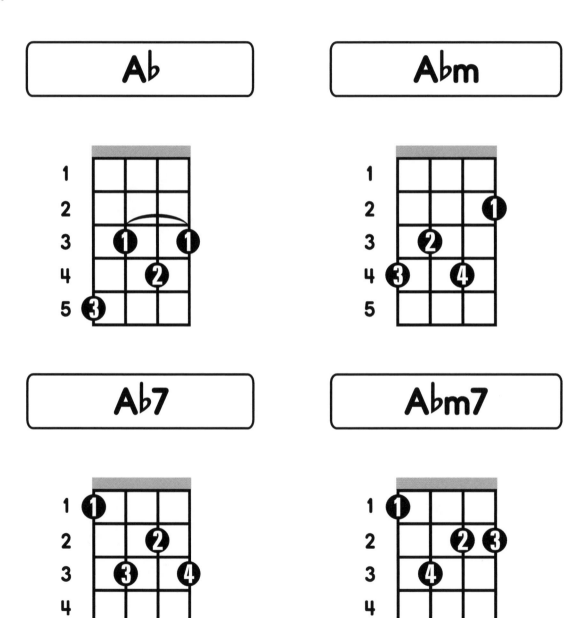

Ab

Abm

Ab7

Abm7

Ab5

Ab6

Abm6

Abmaj7

G# / A♭ Chords

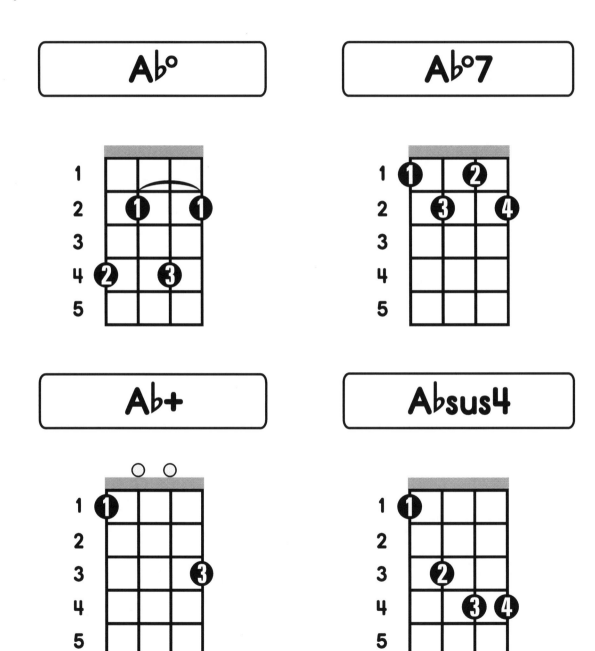

A♭°

A♭°7

A♭+

A♭sus4

A♭add9

A♭madd9

A♭m7-5

A♭7sus4

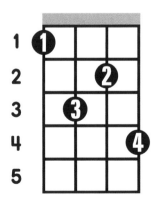

G# / A♭ Chords

A♭sus2

A♭m(maj7)

A♭7-5

A♭7+5

A♭7-9

A♭7+9

A♭-5

A♭9

G# / A♭ Chords

A♭m9

A♭maj9

A♭11

A♭13

A Chords

A Chords

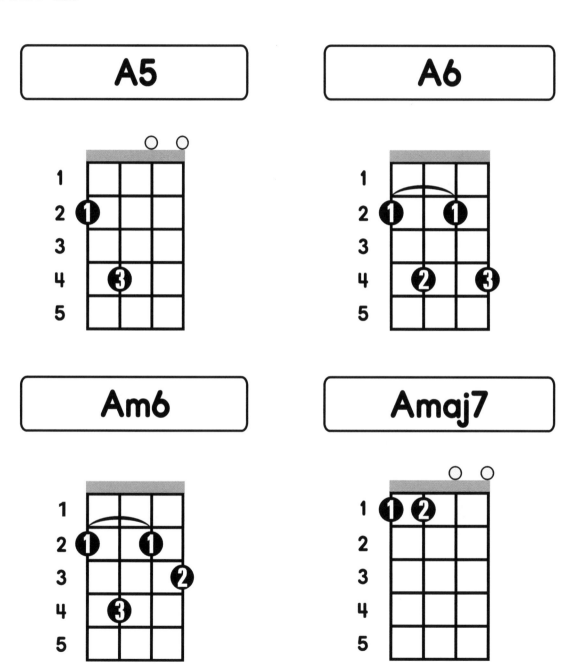

A5

A6

Am6

Amaj7

A Chords

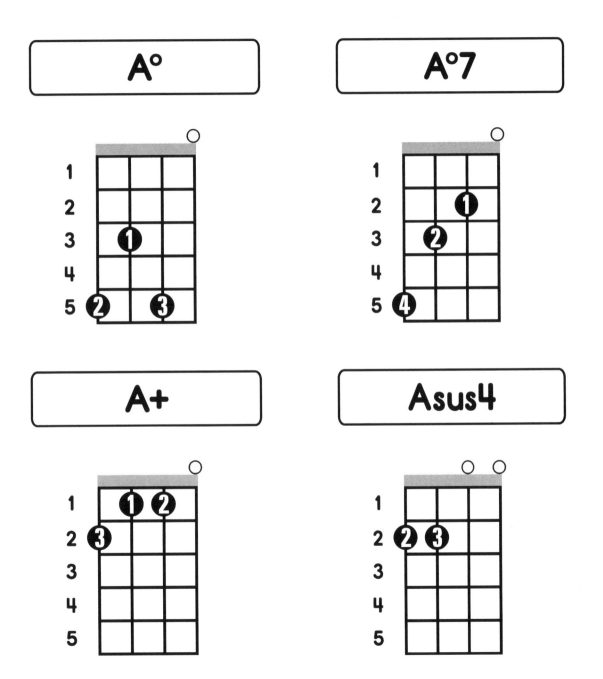

A Chords

Aadd9

Amadd9

Am7-5

A7sus4

A Chords

Asus2

Am(maj7)

A7-5

A7+5

A Chords

A7-9

A7+9

A-5

A9

Am9

Amaj9

A11

A13

A# / B♭ Chords

B♭

B♭m

B♭7

B♭m7

A# / B♭ Chords

B♭5

B♭6

B♭m6

B♭maj7

A# / Bb Chords

Bb°

Bb°7

Bb+

Bbsus4

B♭add9

B♭madd9

B♭m7-5

B♭7sus4

A# / B♭ Chords

B♭sus2

B♭m(maj7)

B♭7-5

B♭7+5

A# / B♭ Chords

B♭7-9

B♭7+9

B♭-5

B♭9

A# / B♭ Chords

B♭m9

B♭maj9

B♭11

B♭13

B Chords

B

Bm

B7

Bm7

B Chords

B Chords

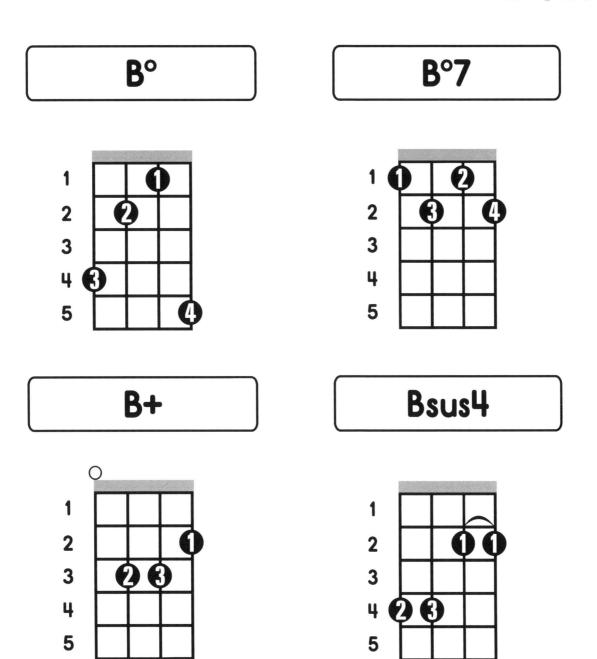

95

B Chords

Badd9

Bmadd9

Bm7-5

B7sus4

Bsus2

Bm(maj7)

(chord diagram)

B7-5

B7+5

B Chords

Bm9

Bmaj9

B11

B13

MOVEABLE CHORDS

What are moveable chords?

A moveable chord is a finger position on the ukulele fingerboard that stays the same even when you move that shape up and down the neck. Figure 1 shows the starting position of **Bb major**. In figure 2 the same chord shape is moved up one fret and the key is changed to **B major**. Figure 3 shows a further progression up the neck to the 3rd fret position and the chord of **C major**.

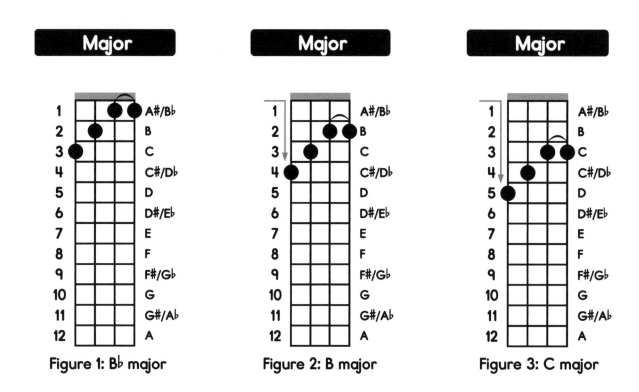

Figure 1: Bb major   Figure 2: B major   Figure 3: C major

The following pages includes a selection of 20 of the most widely used chord types for the ukulele, spread over 48 different examples. Using the examples given, up to 576 different chords are possible depending on the number of frets on your ukulele.

Moveable Chords

Major

1	C#/Db
2	D
3	D#/Eb
4	E
5	F
6	F#/Gb
7	G
8	G#/Ab
9	A
10	A#/Bb
11	B
12	C

Major

1	D#/Eb
2	E
3	F
4	F#/Gb
5	G
6	G#/Ab
7	A
8	A#/Bb
9	B
10	C
11	C#/Db
12	D

Major

1	F#/Gb
2	G
3	G#/Ab
4	A
5	A#/Bb
6	B
7	C
8	C#/Db
9	D
10	D#/Eb
11	E
12	F

Major

1	A#/Bb
2	B
3	C
4	C#/Db
5	D
6	D#/Eb
7	E
8	F
9	F#/Gb
10	G
11	G#/Ab
12	A

Minor

1	D#/Eb
2	E
3	F
4	F#/Gb
5	G
6	G#/Ab
7	A
8	A#/Bb
9	B
10	C
11	C#/Db
12	D

Minor

1	G
2	G#/Ab
3	A
4	A#/Bb
5	B
6	C
7	C#/Db
8	D
9	D#/Eb
10	E
11	F
12	F#/Gb

Moveable Chords

Minor

1	G#/Ab
2	A
3	A#/Bb
4	B
5	C
6	C#/Db
7	D
8	D#/Eb
9	E
10	F
11	F#/Gb
12	G

Minor

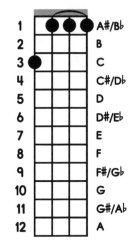

1	A#/Bb
2	B
3	C
4	C#/Db
5	D
6	D#/Eb
7	E
8	F
9	F#/Gb
10	G
11	G#/Ab
12	A

Seventh

1	C#/Db
2	D
3	D#/Eb
4	E
5	F
6	F#/Gb
7	G
8	G#/Ab
9	A
10	A#/Bb
11	B
12	C

Seventh

1	F
2	F#/Gb
3	G
4	G#/Ab
5	A
6	A#/Bb
7	B
8	C
9	C#/Db
10	D
11	D#/Eb
12	E

Seventh

1	G#/Ab
2	A
3	A#/Bb
4	B
5	C
6	C#/Db
7	D
8	D#/Eb
9	E
10	F
11	F#/Gb
12	G

Seventh

1	A#/Bb
2	B
3	C
4	C#/Db
5	D
6	D#/Eb
7	E
8	F
9	F#/Gb
10	G
11	G#/Ab
12	A

Moveable Chords

Minor Seventh

1		D
2		D#/Eb
3		E
4		F
5		F#/Gb
6		G
7		G#/Ab
8		A
9		A#/Bb
10		B
11		C
12		C#/Db

Minor Seventh

1		F
2		F#/Gb
3		G
4		G#/Ab
5		A
6		A#/Bb
7		B
8		C
9		C#/Db
10		D
11		D#/Eb
12		E

Minor Seventh

1		G#/Ab
2		A
3		A#/Bb
4		B
5		C
6		C#/Db
7		D
8		D#/Eb
9		E
10		F
11		F#/Gb
12		G

Minor Seventh

1		A#/Bb
2		B
3		C
4		C#/Db
5		D
6		D#/Eb
7		E
8		F
9		F#/Gb
10		G
11		G#/Ab
12		A

Sixth

1		C#/Db
2		D
3		D#/Eb
4		E
5		F
6		F#/Gb
7		G
8		G#/Ab
9		A
10		A#/Bb
11		B
12		C

Sixth

1		F
2		F#/Gb
3		G
4		G#/Ab
5		A
6		A#/Bb
7		B
8		C
9		C#/Db
10		D
11		D#/Eb
12		E

Moveable Chords

Sixth

Fret	Note
1	G#/Ab
2	A
3	A#/Bb
4	B
5	C
6	C#/Db
7	D
8	D#/Eb
9	E
10	F
11	F#/Gb
12	G

Sixth

Fret	Note
1	B
2	C
3	C#/Db
4	D
5	D#/Eb
6	E
7	F
8	F#/Gb
9	G
10	G#/Ab
11	A
12	A#/Bb

Minor Sixth

Fret	Note
1	D
2	D#/Eb
3	E
4	F
5	F#/Gb
6	G
7	G#/Ab
8	A
9	A#/Bb
10	B
11	C
12	C#/Db

Minor Sixth

Fret	Note
1	F
2	F#/Gb
3	G
4	G#/Ab
5	A
6	A#/Bb
7	B
8	C
9	C#/Db
10	D
11	D#/Eb
12	E

Minor Sixth

Fret	Note
1	G#/Ab
2	A
3	A#/Bb
4	B
5	C
6	C#/Db
7	D
8	D#/Eb
9	E
10	F
11	F#/Gb
12	G

Minor Sixth

Fret	Note
1	B
2	C
3	C#/Db
4	D
5	D#/Eb
6	E
7	F
8	F#/Gb
9	G
10	G#/Ab
11	A
12	A#/Bb

Moveable Chords

Major Seventh

1	C#/Db
2	D
3	D#/Eb
4	E
5	F
6	F#/Gb
7	G
8	G#/Ab
9	A
10	A#/Bb
11	B
12	C

Major Seventh

1	F
2	F#/Gb
3	G
4	G#/Ab
5	A
6	A#/Bb
7	B
8	C
9	C#/Db
10	D
11	D#/Eb
12	E

Major Seventh

1	B
2	C
3	C#/Db
4	D
5	D#/Eb
6	E
7	F
8	F#/Gb
9	G
10	G#/Ab
11	A
12	A#/Bb

Suspended Fourth

1	C#/Db
2	D
3	D#/Eb
4	E
5	F
6	F#/Gb
7	G
8	G#/Ab
9	A
10	A#/Bb
11	B
12	C

Suspended Fourth

1	D#/Eb
2	E
3	F
4	F#/Gb
5	G
6	G#/Ab
7	A
8	A#/Bb
9	B
10	C
11	C#/Db
12	D

Suspended Fourth

1	A#/Bb
2	B
3	C
4	C#/Db
5	D
6	D#/Eb
7	E
8	F
9	F#/Gb
10	G
11	G#/Ab
12	A

Moveable Chords

Diminished

1	D
2	D#/E♭
3	E
4	F
5	F#/G♭
6	G
7	G#/A♭
8	A
9	A#/B♭
10	B
11	C
12	C#/D♭

Diminished

1	G
2	G#/A♭
3	A
4	A#/B♭
5	B
6	C
7	C#/D♭
8	D
9	D#/E♭
10	E
11	F
12	F#/G♭

Diminished

1	G
2	G#/A♭
3	A
4	A#/B♭
5	B
6	C
7	C#/D♭
8	D
9	D#/E♭
10	E
11	F
12	F#/G♭

Augmented

1	D
2	D#/E♭
3	E
4	F
5	F#/G♭
6	G
7	G#/A♭
8	A
9	A#/B♭
10	B
11	C
12	C#/D♭

Augmented

1	F
2	F#/G♭
3	G
4	G#/A♭
5	A
6	A#/B♭
7	B
8	C
9	C#/D♭
10	D
11	D#/E♭
12	E

Augmented

1	A#/B♭
2	B
3	C
4	C#/D♭
5	D
6	D#/E♭
7	E
8	F
9	F#/G♭
10	G
11	G#/A♭
12	A

Moveable Chords

Diminished Seventh

1	D
2	D#/Eb
3	E
4	F
5	F#/Gb
6	G
7	G#/Ab
8	A
9	A#/Bb
10	B
11	C
12	C#/Db

Diminished Seventh

1	F
2	F#/Gb
3	G
4	G#/Ab
5	A
6	A#/Bb
7	B
8	C
9	C#/Db
10	D
11	D#/Eb
12	E

Fifth

1	C#/Db
2	D
3	D#/Eb
4	E
5	F
6	F#/Gb
7	G
8	G#/Ab
9	A
10	A#/Bb
11	B
12	C

Fifth

1	G#/Ab
2	A
3	A#/Bb
4	B
5	C
6	C#/Db
7	D
8	D#/Eb
9	E
10	F
11	F#/Gb
12	G

Seventh Suspended

1	C#/Db
2	D
3	D#/Eb
4	E
5	F
6	F#/Gb
7	G
8	G#/Ab
9	A
10	A#/Bb
11	B
12	C

Added Ninth

1	F#/Gb
2	G
3	G#/Ab
4	A
5	A#/Bb
6	B
7	C
8	C#/Db
9	D
10	D#/Eb
11	E
12	F

Moveable Chords

Added Ninth

		A#/Bb
1		A#/Bb
2		B
3		C
4		C#/Db
5		D
6		D#/Eb
7		E
8		F
9		F#/Gb
10		G
11		G#/Ab
12		A

Ninth

		A
1		A
2		A#/Bb
3		B
4		C
5		C#/Db
6		D
7		D#/Eb
8		E
9		F
10		F#/Gb
11		G
12		G#/Ab

Minor Ninth

		A#/Bb
1		A#/Bb
2		B
3		C
4		C#/Db
5		D
6		D#/Eb
7		E
8		F
9		F#/Gb
10		G
11		G#/Ab
12		A

Major Ninth

		A
1		A
2		A#/Bb
3		B
4		C
5		C#/Db
6		D
7		D#/Eb
8		E
9		F
10		F#/Gb
11		G
12		G#/Ab

Eleventh

		F#/Gb
1		F#/Gb
2		G
3		G#/Ab
4		A
5		A#/Bb
6		B
7		C
8		C#/Db
9		D
10		D#/Eb
11		E
12		F

Thirteenth

		C#/Db
1		C#/Db
2		D
3		D#/Eb
4		E
5		F
6		F#/Gb
7		G
8		G#/Ab
9		A
10		A#/Bb
11		B
12		C

Further ukulele family publications from Cabot Books

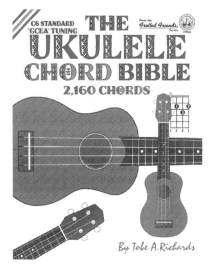

FF08 The Ukulele Chord Bible: C6 Standard Tuning (GCEA) 2,160 Chords
(ISBN 13: 978-1-906207-29-8)

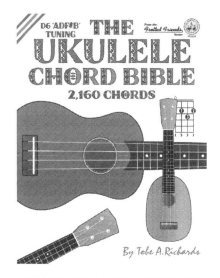

FF23 The Ukulele Chord Bible: D6 Tuning (ADF#B) 2,160 Chords
(ISBN 13: 978-1-906207-44-1)

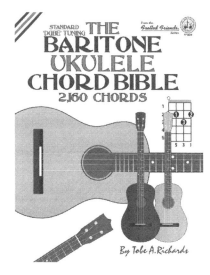

FF10 The Baritone Ukulele Chord Bible: Standard G6 Tuning (DGBE) 2,160 Chords
(ISBN 13: 978-1-906207-31-1)

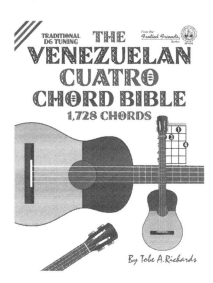

FF11 The Venezuelan Cuatro Chord Bible: Standard Tuning (ADF#B) 1,728 Chords
(ISBN 13: 978-1-906207-32-8)

FF08 The Cavaquinho Chord Bible: Standard DGBD Tuning 1,728 Chords
(ISBN 13: 978-1-906207-39-7)

FF02 The Charango Chord Bible Traditional GCEAE Tuning 1,728 Chords
(ISBN 13: 978-1-906207-23-6)

Guitar family publications from Cabot Books

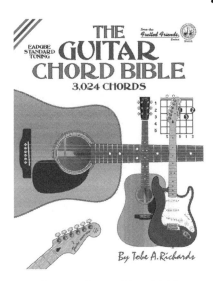

FF35 The Guitar Chord Bible: Standard Tuning 3,024 Chords (ISBN 13: 978-1-906207-55-7)

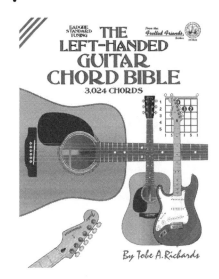

FF36 The Left-Handed Guitar Chord Bible: Standard Tuning 3,024 Chords (ISBN 13: 978-1-906207-56-4)

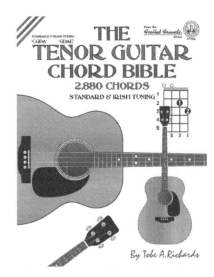

FF16 The Tenor Guitar Chord Bible: Standard & Irish Tuning 2,880 Chords (ISBN 13: 978-1-906207-35-9)

FF31 The Baritone Guitar Chord Bible: Low B Tuning 1,728 Chords (ISBN 13: 978-1-906207-50-2)

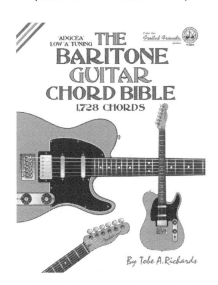

FF33 The Baritone Guitar Chord Bible: Low A Tuning 1,728 Chords (ISBN 13: 978-1-906207-52-6)

FF30 The Requinto Chord Bible: Standard Tuning 1,728 Chords (ISBN 13: 978-1-906207-49-6)

Made in United States
Orlando, FL
27 June 2022

19215870R00061